A
Bitter
Pacifist

Beatriz Trana
Copyright © 2017Beatriz Trana

ISBN-13: 978-0-692-99094-0

A
Bitter
Pacifist

Beatriz Trana

This book is for my ten year old self that thought she would've been dead by now.

CONTENTS

LOVE

What thoughts and memories fit into your version of love?

Hopeless romance of a child
is filled with purity and innocence,
immaturity and coincidence reside.

Hopeless romance of an adolescent
is excitingly scary, new, and more sexual.
To then be heartbroken,
making one feel blue and psychosexual.

Hopeless romance of an adult
is flickering light.
Flickering hope then despair, hope then despair
how does one cope with this nightmare.

I don't understand you
nobody does
but why have you touched everyones heart
except mine.

It's amazing how his gaze
kills my heart.

Yet
revives my soul,
suffocating my body.

Til the end of my obliteration
is perfect.

At a time like this
swear that you'll take care of me.
Stare at me and declare it to me.

Promise you'll be my honey bear,
and be there for me.

Honey,

Let us steal a corvette,
and smoke a cigarette.

Let us go to Paris,
and kiss on the hotel terrace.

Let us make love on a dozen roses,
and go into psychosis.

Taking heroin doses
we die in the ocean.

Thank you
for giving me that one second rush.
It wasn't much but it was enough
to wake me up

Write me a love song.

Tell me you'll hold me.
Tell me you'll take me away.

Away from me and my mind
just for one day.

Make me want to stay.

He stared at me
With his blueberry eyes.
He puckered his red apple lips.
He touched me with his silky sinner skin.
He came in for the win.

Not knowing I was the girl he used to call pig skin,
I kicked him in the shin.

If you wish me to pretend a smile,
I shall smile.
If you wish me to lie,
I shall lie.
If you wish to hit me,
I shall be hit.

I know you're not the one,
But it's better than none.

Art is my form of therapy
it's an ancient remedy,
it's not my enemy,
it's my beautiful Penelope.

She's extraordinarily necessary
for my mental security.

"Why can't I have you ?" I said.
You laugh.

"I love you." I said.
You drove.

"I need you." I said.
You leave me to bleed.

I already know
this will be another one of those nights.
If only he knew
I lived for him.
It's too late now
The actions won't agree to be takin back
nor do I want to give them back.
My eyes cry dry.
bye bye
my love.

Scare me.
I need to feel something,
like your bare hands on my skin.
I need to feel something,
like the veins that run up and down your forearms.
I need to feel something,
like your broad shoulders on a gloomy day,
like your manly hands on my neck,
like your eyes that fraternize with mine.
I need
to feel
something with you
again.

Leaves sway
you take my breath away.

Grass grows
you take off my clothes.

Flowers blossom
this feels awesome.

Water flows
as we discompose.

Natures a beaut
we are absolute.

Thinking of you brings me so much fucking pain.

You know what I don't care.
I've lost all my flare.
I cried till despair.
lets go elsewhere,
and start an affair.

Confusing thing as a child,
sought after in adolescence,
part of life as an adult,
reminisced as an elder.

Sex,
the drug of choice.

We search for the act even if we don't
care for it,
flare for it,
stare at it,
we prepare for it.
Our minds are at constant warfare with it.

Sex,
the drug of choice.

The films along with the
magazines and fantasies,
the fact of the act
we knack that we need the act.

Sex,
the drug of choice.

Why can't I have you,
I love you.

You make me so happy,
I get so sappy.

You seem so edgy and free, so
I envy and flee.

I say I'm pretty when I cry,
You say I'm pretty when I die.

I say come on baby light my fire,
you say come on baby your a liar.

- Lana & Jim

What a groovy place to trip
with people that are hip.
Dancing around bare
with no cares.
California 1969
What a groovy time
to be alive.

Your such a beautiful mystic creature.
You brought so much joy where ever you went.
You showed me what joy meant.
The time I spent with you I'll never repent

For Veronica

SADNESS

Is it a fad to feel sad?

What a dumb life I've lived.
It makes me feel like scum.
The only way to make it numb
is to drink some rum.

I miss those nights where we'd lay beside each other looking at one another shedding tears on the bed.

Thinking of what life would be like ahead.
Thinking of what it would be like to be dead.

I really do miss you knuckles head.

For Alexis

They told her to do it,
so she did it.

I choke when I think of you. I choke with the feelings of happiness when my mind shows me visions of us being happy, laughing, enjoying our youth, succumbing to old age together. I choke with the feelings of sadness, because I know, I know. You don't see me, you don't know who I am, you don't need me. My eyes water when I choke with these feelings. My eyes water, because I can't live with them anymore. These feelings you make me feel, stab me and stab me with so much agony. It desolates me. I wish you never existed. I cry, cry and cry morning after morning, night after night. I cry, because I will not grow old with you. I cry because you chose the other girl. My body, mind, and soul died because all I needed was you.

Sometimes the nights are tough
I think I've had enough.

I put on a gown
and lay down.
To
countdown
the let downs,
countdown
the meltdowns,
countdown
the days left in this small town.

Fillmore, CA

Dear "best friend",

I hurt my wrists all these years. I cried all these years. I told you I was ready to die every year. But, you never heard me. You never helped me. You never hugged me to reassure me I was gonna live a life full of happiness. You made new friends. You didn't bother to say goodbye. So, I left. I ran. I fled. I bled and bled for years. No matter what I did you couldn't even give one second out of your fun fucking filled life, for your so called "best friend".

Farewell,
you pest of a friend

For Katia

Thank you for not telling me it was just a phase.

I show you my work but,

You don't even bat an eye
that makes me want to die.

You don't even lend me your ears
do you even know I'm here.

Should I just disappear.

What did I do?
Confused, my brain feels abused.
I wonder why but I'm
accused and bruised.
I always wondered why it
made you so amused.

How does one not run out of tears?
Better yet why can't I run out of tears?

I know I'll never be special,
I understand that now.
Through those seven years not once
did you regret daughter deprecation day.
I sat there taking it all in.
You shout.
Repulsive pig take off that wig!
Dumb piece of gum on my shoe, you're scum!
I get it, I get it, I get it
just
stop, stop, stop please for the love of god stop!
bang, bang, bang
skull opened
I fell and I yell.
Just another story for show and tell.

For Mother

Drowning with my life vest
I resist death.

Mourning for Morrison.
Piaf takes a drag.
My hearts stop'n for Joplin.
Hendrix laughs.
Holy moly I miss Bowie.

For Jim, Edith, Janis, Jimi, & David

I think so much,
I forget to blink.

DEPRESSION

How long did your depression last?

9/22/2010
"i tried to suicide myself"

- the innocence

It's coming,
It's coming again.
Please
make it stop.
My chest
it begins to feel weight.
I can't breath.
I don't want this feeling to last.
This feeling I hate it, I hate it, I hate it!
My feet volunteer and walk
to the chains at the end of my bed.
My ankles hurt my wrists hurt
I can't take this anymore.
I don't want to cry but I cry.
What sorrow I feel
I feel hate towards it.
I fight.
It stands strong.
what do I do?
tell me
please,
this agony
I've had enough.
But, it still comes
to me
it comes.

Its coming again
please,
make it stop.

My bed is the only one there
to hug me when these suicide impulses are so strong.
They paralyze me
gripping and squeezing
my chest, my heart, my liver, my brain,
everything
all night long.
I am no longer strong.

Sometimes I thought my room was my prison.
Sometimes I thought my room was my friend.
Sometimes I thought my room wanted me dead.

Sometimes I wake up and realize I wish I didn't
have to think about the relationship between me
and my room.

Sometimes I just wish I could've had normal teenage
thoughts, like I wish prom was at sea or lets go
hangout under that big tree.

Doing the same routines
over and over again.
Doing the same things
over an over again.

Tends to bring
feelings of beatings and dealings,
that stings and clings
to our beings.

Being numb is a lifestyle
I forced myself to live in. To see if I could
be stronger and not feel so conquered by this life
thats always treated me like a monster.

It's 3 A.M.
The voices come out to play.
Cigarette buds scratch my skin away.
I become an ashtray,
when all I ever wanted to be was a Blue Jay.

Instead of moving
ahead.
I stayed in
bed,
till I bled
knowing
I've been dead.

No one is here
I hug myself,
because
no one is here.

No one is here
to stop me.
I strangle myself
still no one is here.

The hands clench up.
The chest inflicts pain unto itself.
The body curls up.
The eyes then produce tears.
The pain is unbearable.
The brains thoughts are unbearable.
The death, the death is bearable.

In these four walls I shed tears.
On the cold hardwood floors I fall.
The person in the mirror I despise.
What can I do to fix these cries.
should I sleep with guys,
no that's not wise.
Should I put on a disguise
no, no more lies.
Or should I chant to the skies
to make me rise.
What do you advise?

A rose
that abodes in thorns.

A glimpse of light
in a shadow of dark.

A last line of cocaine
that didn't go down the drain.

A little rain
on a scorching day.

Are you a optimistic or pessimistic?

Why can't I talk to you?
Why cant I talk to anyone?
Just once, participate in a conversation of any
occasion.

Why do I freeze up?
Why cant I move?
Just once, participate in an action with compassion.

Why do I stare at you?
Why do I observe people?
Just once, talk and interlock connections with a flock.

I'm tired.
You bring me down
treat me like a clown
I frown.
Driving downtown
to end it all.
I drown.

Yellow, blue, red,
Oh wow did I say blue I meant green,
what a dazey dream
makes me forget the color scheme.

Is it a dream?

Green herb superb,
My parents kick me to the curb
while alcohol perturbs.

The drugs hug my brain
to regulate the pain and make me sane.
My parents disdain
while I slowly detrain
the dazey train ride I pertained.

My family reminds me that I'm useless everyday
even the streets whisper it to me.

I wish they could fade away.

Oh black void of nothingness
how I've become accustomed to your presence.

You don't haunt me you
accompany me.

You greet me everyday.
You sleep with me every night.

We've grown to be good friends
when once it didn't make sense.

Your wit is quick possibly slick
makes my will to live a
wick that fails to flick.

I thrived
to live a mere life
full of strife.

It's a house
decorated with depression,
scented with anger,
haunted by sadness,
and filled with numb people.

Happy Birthday!

You were born to be
torn, scorned, then mourned.

Your heart potent
to then be broken.

Your body so gentle it's a temple
waiting to dissemble.

Your soul so strong
to then not respond.

You were born to be
torn, scorned, then mourned.

Happy Birthday!

I guess depression really does suck the life out of you

Her nose was dripping red.
While the rain drip dropped on her head,
and her life was hanging by a thread.

Depression,
is a disorder too many people know too well.

ANGER

My anger is an intruder, is yours?

You don't read my poems because they make you sad
what a lad.

Sorry I'm not happy
and yappy.

Filled with sunshine
and white wine.

I live depressed and stressed,
repressed in house arrest.

Filled with moonshine
and red wine.

"You're so insensitive" she says.
stop! being so hypersensitive.

You're not a princess,
you're a mess.

Making my life a slugfest,
just give it a rest
don't be a pest.

Why are all the sheep so cruel?

Why oh why must I be the lone wolf
dressed as the sheep.
Why oh why can't I be the wolf
who cuts the throat of the sheep nice and deep
with my teeth.
Wait! let me breath and weep
while I watch the blood slowly seep
into my paradoxical sleep.

When I hurt you,
just know you hurt me ten times more
then I ever could.

I never understood why I chose to hurt myself over and over again by getting excited of the thought of making new friends. Clearly, all their attention is saved for their phones and their brain rotting apps why can't they just relax and not relapse

"you're so innocent and sweet,
incapable of dark thoughts or messing with an upside
down cross"

What a cold sore you are
a whore who speaks bore.
Son of a motherless goat
go die by strep throat.

I lived in that place not to be named, for seven years.
The eyes suggest me to change.
I never wanted to change
looking like them would be so lame.
I hate this place that would not be named.
Biological eyes are so blind,
enucleate them I would if I could.

Forget me.
I'm not your marionette.
you upset me.
I hope I can reset.

I am fucking done with the idiocracy of the world.
I am done with the idiots, the assholes, and the
ignorant.

I'll gladly tie my noose and
I'll gladly step off that chair.
I'll gladly leave this fucking world
that so clearly doesn't care.

What have I done to you.
What have I done to upset you.

Whatever it may be I truly am sorry I ever met you.

I just wanted a friend.
I just wanted to know
what it felt like to have a friendship.

I know now they all have a bitter end.
I know now it's all just pretend.

You were the biggest bully ever bestowed upon me.
You bullied me then forgot about it
making myself believe I'm crazy.
You gave me a friend, a friend who taught me how to
live and you took her, you took her away from me,
making myself know you are crazy.

For Hector

For one second in this lifetime
I thought you were different.
I thought wrong.
System haunts from these results
all hopes are drawn.

My head hurts.
Emotions get dry as deserts.

Do you think your an expert on me.
I'm not a class you take for one year
you damn flea.
I wish I could break our knee
and watch you beg for your leg.

Honestly, just fuck off.
Leave me alone with solitude,
she is the only one who has stuck around.
She's painful even baneful but she stays faithful.

You lay down so sad,
makes me so mad
your'e a deadbeat dad.
Go be a nomad,
get unsad
my fellow comrade.

For Dad

Why do I hate you.
Is it because you remind me
of what I could be if it wasn't for anxiety.

Damn you! anxiety personality.
my loyalty to you makes me miss out
on the entirety of humanity.

You silently become a monstrosity.
My sanity decreases,
leading to a fatality
in my mentality.

"Friends" suck.
Finding them I've never had luck,
But when I do
they're drunks,
they're schmucks
who smell like skunk.
"Friends" suck.
I hope they get hit by a truck.

The sheep tell you its gonna be okay,
the feeling won't stay.
The sheep tell you they know what you go through,
so no need to feel blue.

But they don't help, they don't even know you.

Maybe all the sheep should just be put to sleep.

I
RAN
OUT
OF LIFE

short story

It is 3:00 am on December 7, 2017. I don't have much time to tell you my story, we probably have ten-fifteen minutes, so let us begin. It all started in 2012, I was 11 years old and lived near a beautiful beach named Newport. I could wake up and smell the ocean air , feel the silky breeze , and see the blue tinted sky through my car sized windows. I had everything you could have wished for. You'd imagine I'd be a happy person but I wasn't. I didn't greet, talk, nor reply to questions as simple as "what's your name". I could tell that people thought I was rude but in reality I was just too scared and paralyzed by my anxiety that I couldn't wave a hello or simply open my mouth to say "My name is violet clément." My parents were furious that I wasn't a normal social human being. Never did they realize it was anxiety. In their world anxiety does not exist, it's not even a concept. Only weak people can have mental health issues like anxiety or depression. If only they knew that their daughter was probably the most weakest girl in the universe. Many years passed and I woke up again to the same routine. smelling the ocean, feeling the breeze, and seeing the blue tinted sky only this time it was accompanied by the yells of my parents. Yelling about why they're pathetic and why each of them should go to hell but that was all normal to me now. After listening to that everyday for breakfast, lunch, and dinner who wouldn't get accustomed. What did scare me was that my blue tinted skies weren't blue they were gray, but I guess the gray sky came with a package deal of loneliness and depression because I was feeling those as well. Now I did say I grew accustomed to my parents yelling but, I didn't get accustomed to the fact they were blaming me for all their problems. For example, why they lost their job, why they're in debt, why their back hurts, why, why, why, and why. The list never ended not till this day either. It's a lot of strain on a 14 year old I was barely starting high school and I lost my first best friend because I was causing her too much emotional fatigue. I don't blame her, who would want to listen to the same person's problems for years. I also wasn't much fun or pretty to look at, but it did hurt because she was my only friend for 7 years. I had forgotten how to make them and I didn't have the courage to do so.

That takes us to the second reason why I did what I did. School, that includes elementary, middle school, and high school. All three of those separate hells were actual hell.

Elementary, I made my friend, my only friend (yes the best friend that left me, that's her). Then declare my love to a boy who we shall not name, and he proceeds to call me "fat ugly pig". Not to great for a nine year old's self esteem especially, because she goes home everyday to hear that from her parents. Middle school, I had no friends throughout the whole two years! My grades began to fail, my thoughts began to talk to me, my soul slowly deteriorated, and my sky wasn't grey anymore it was black. I'm guessing it turned black because the depression was making itself comfortable. Still hasn't gone anywhere to this day. High school, I could not endure public high school, for two years. so I managed to do independent studies. Throughout those two years my grades were absolutely awful but, I did manage to take some of my emotions and transfer them into paintings, poems, and short films. The only problem I was facing, was that I had no one to show them to. No one to experience my work, I was so proud of making. No one supported me. I found something that brought a bit of blue back into my sky. But, no one helped me bring back the entirety of blue to all of my sky. Quickly making the little bit of blue I had fade away.

Leading us to the final reason, friends. I was attending independent studies, that didn't mean I was homeschooled, although now that I think about it that would've been better, I still went to a little building for an hour to turn in homework. A miracle happened one day I was waiting to be picked up and, a girl came up to me saying she wanted to be friends. Immediately, I thought of a million excuses of telling her why I couldn't be her friend but, something clicked in my brain and the friendship began. It was strange at first but then it got interesting and I got to hear all of her wild experiences, aspirations, and fears. We got at a state where I believed we were comfortable enough that I could show her some of my work, so I did. One by one I showed her and she expressed nothing. Then she said "they're okay since you're only beginning but your style isn't my favorite". I was devastated I thought she was a friend. I thought she would support me, she doesn't have to like my work, just support me and tell me she was

101

happy that I found something that brought me joy. That's what a true friend would do after all. I was proud of my work but I was too weak, and her lack of support stuck with me. I was so happy I made a friend again that I just smiled and agreed with her but, I was so furious. I lost her as a friend too.

Well here we are back at square one no self esteem, no friends, no happiness. I tried to make more friends but I didn't manage to keep the friendships healthy they all rotted. I tried to make more art but I began to think to myself. Who am I making these for? myself, I hate myself. I don't deserve anything. Then I tried to get along with my parents. They still treated me like a sewer rat. But, the saddest part was that my sky never turned blue. My sky remained black. It will never turn black.

Now a bit of background before I tell you this last part and the void of eternal sleep takes me away. Throughout these years my mind was not sane I had psychopathic thoughts as well as suicidal thoughts. so, I created a list of how I would want to leave this world. Most include dying in water, and if you forgot I live near the beach so, that was convenient. I don't know why, water? I've just always felt like I was flying through heavenly clouds when I swam. Watching my dress dance underwater and feeling weightless tied to nothing, no one, or anything. Well, fellow stranger the time has come it's 3:11am on December 7th I only have about four minutes left If you still don't realize what I did well, just imagine a 16 year old girl walking into the ocean leaving a trail of red along with her footsteps.

I hold no grudge towards anyone not even my parents. Most importantly I didn't die filled with hate or sadness. This felt right from the very beginning, never regretting my decision. I hope you have a wonderful life full of joy and laughter.

With the bit of love I have left ,

Violet Clément

merci.

ABOUT THE BOOK

A Bitter Pacifist is about Beatriz Trana's struggle with depression. It's categorized in four sections love, sadness, depression, and anger. Which signify the only four emotions that she felt during her dark times. It's a book filled with agony and affliction. It's a great book all can relate to.